From the Forgotten World into Eternity

Poetry by Beren Maximus

Illustrations by
Inés de Castro
Ted Nasmith
Dalibor Zlatkovic

Garnet Star Publishing

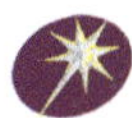

Cover art: *Tinuvyel Reborn* by Ted Nasmith

First edition 2012 by Schiel & Denver Publishing Ltd.
Second edition 2014 by Garnet Star Publishing, Boston
Revised and enhanced

ISBN 978-0-9907504-0-6 (sc)
ISBN 978-0-9907504-4-4 ebook
ISBN 978-0-9907504-3-7 (sc Srpski)

Library of Congress Control Number: 2014949461

Printed in the United States of America

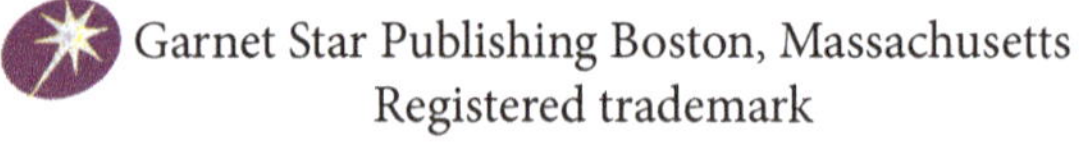
Garnet Star Publishing Boston, Massachusetts
Registered trademark

Praise for
From the Forgotten World Into Eternity

Milorad's poetry is clearly the product of a talented wordsmith and a deeply spiritual and aesthetic soul. His words entice you into a realm of soothing enchantment and beauty, yet not without sadness and poignancy. He offers respite to harried modern readers burdened with the stress and antagonisms of daily life, not unlike the imaginary lands of Middle-earth so many of us also love to visit in our minds. His meditations on love in particular recall the great Rumi. —*Ted Nasmith*

This book is quite beautiful. The verses touched me and the illustrations are other worldly. It reminds me of Kahlil Gibran.—*J. Goddard, U.K.*

The author has a beautiful gift that he shares without any pretense—it is pure and good, straight from the heart! Very soothing yet thought provoking.—*Marilyn M.*

Very lovely ... and the paintings too ... Tinuviyel is a lucky girl!—*Jenetta C.*

"If only I can leave a little bit of me behind that is my very best, as a tiny seed that may grow richly in a blessing of Love. When this time comes, when I will be long gone from this form, I think my prayers will have been answered."

— *Inés de Castro*

Contents

Foreword

There comes a time when the soul sends you its signal of awakening.

It is often very silent and gentle, almost unheard and most of the time neglected.

But when you hear it, taste it and fully absorb it, then it happens:

The miracle of you.

A long time ago in an age long forgotten there was a world where light and darkness twisted their own stories among human beings.

And from that world I bring you memories, sufferings, joy, sadness but most of all — Love.

Love — that power of endless life and change.

And now it comes from that long forgotten world, reaching into eternity.

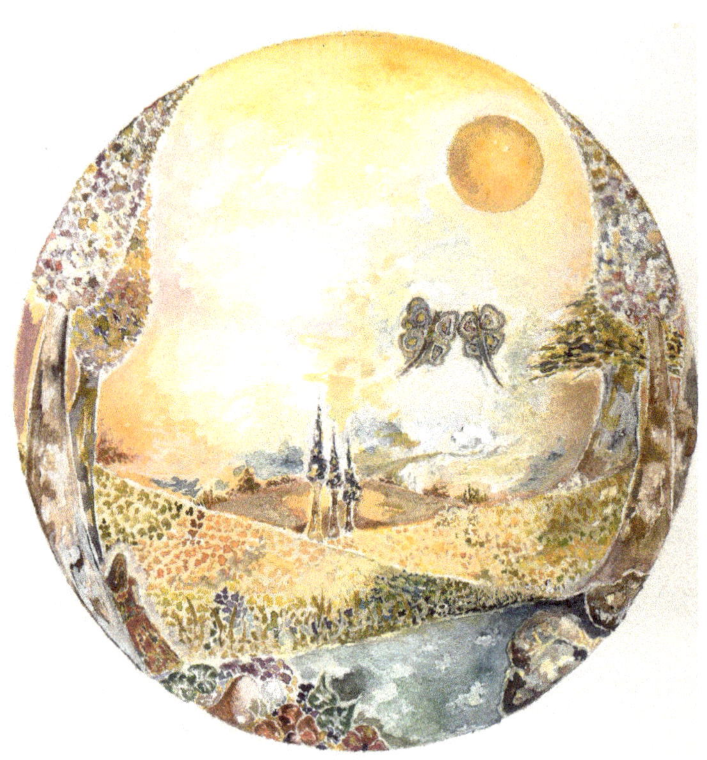

Le Passage, by Inés de Castro

Ancient Mariners

We are sailing through this life
on the sea waves …

The sea of love and hate,
which we understand not.

Roaring thunders in darkest nights
and heavy rain veils.

When our feet feel the Earth again,
we will thank the heavens above.

So thus we sail …

Our Home

Our home is where beauty springs.
Flowers are everywhere
and their scent is making you smile.
Every time.
But we are not in our home now,
we are led away, far away …
into places without name …

Our home was filled with nightingale's tune
and heavenly harps …
Our road is now full of racket and noise …
killing our hearts.

We can't live in a place where we are bound,
where our souls are silently crying …
We do not belong there.
Born into eternity—but it was stolen from us,
made us dying …

We are deeply cared for and loved
but persuaded and lured into lies instead.
instead of roses and lilies
we have now a dreadful bed ...

Oh how I long for my eternal home ...
It is not made of wood or stone ...

Oh how I yearn to see my friends again!
Beautiful souls beyond any words ... again ...

Where are you now my Tinuviyel?
Did morning dew bring you my kisses,
before the sunrise?

Oh how I yearn for home ...

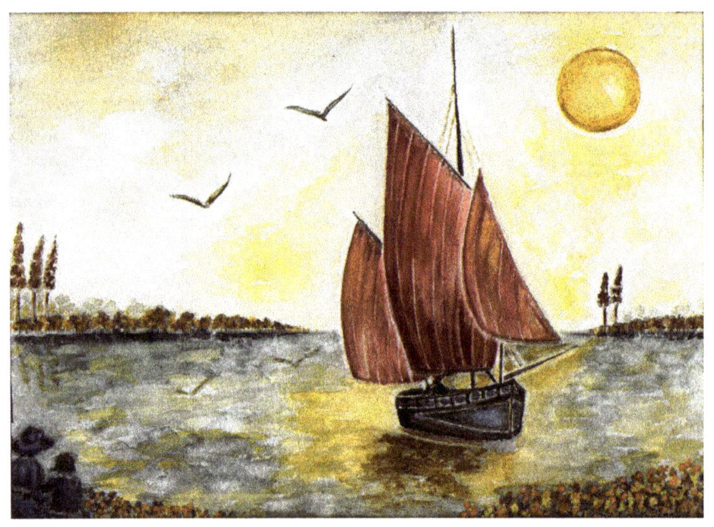

Conversation en bord de mer, by Inés de Castro

Memory of Beauty

Summer breeze was meant to be,
to tease your arms and the palm of your left hand
where you held a rose for me.

And Birches are singing in a memory of you
swinging mightily, following lightly
your trace imprinted in the ether—in truth.

Your hair would burn the wind,
when dancing alone behind the pale trees
in the forests of old,

where I first saw you …

Where my heart always returns
to sing our song and dance our tune
Of our love and our truth …

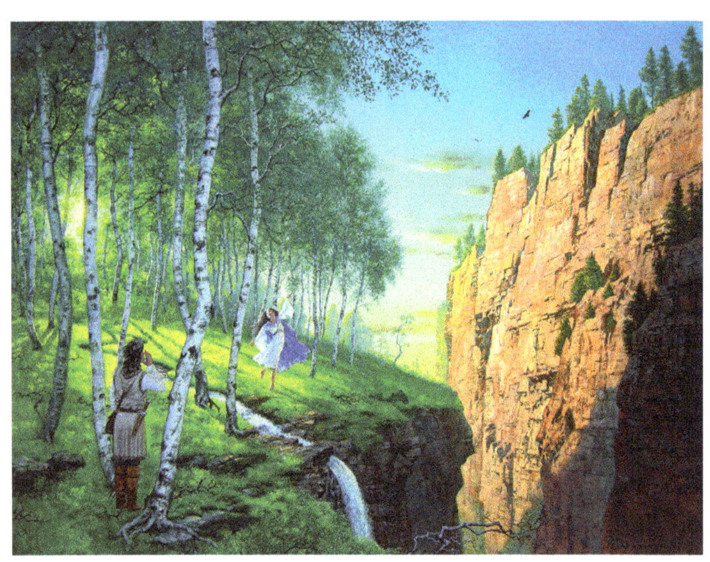

Tinuviyel Reborn, by Ted Nasmith

Somewhere in Time

I saw your hands, I felt your lips …
I saw light in your eyes.
Somewhere in time I was alive …

Gazing deeply into two jewels
Standing, I was on the brink of the world
and was not afraid.

Your words I felt within me …
Shining waves of energy …
I swam across.

Now
if there is a thing called now,
I return to you
and call your name in the forests of the universe …

O Lutien!
O Tinuviyel!

God's Children

The bright light of new morning
is waking me up, raising my eyes.

And sounds of birds singing …

The Colors of the day are violet and gold
mixed in the dew, making the perfect mold.

Of unity of the living …

I am alone or so I thought.
Spread over the moss and flowers beneath.
Sinking low in my mind
and flying high on the ray of Love.

Then I saw you …
Then I heard your divine voice.
Then I kissed your lips
for you are my everlasting choice.

Tinuviyel, my only fair
living beauty, upon the land
and all across the universe,
wherever your feet stand.

Ah!
Blessed be the new light and Love that spreads over,
forever here shining bright, and wonders that
uncover our hearts and our souls,
as God's children, truly loved.

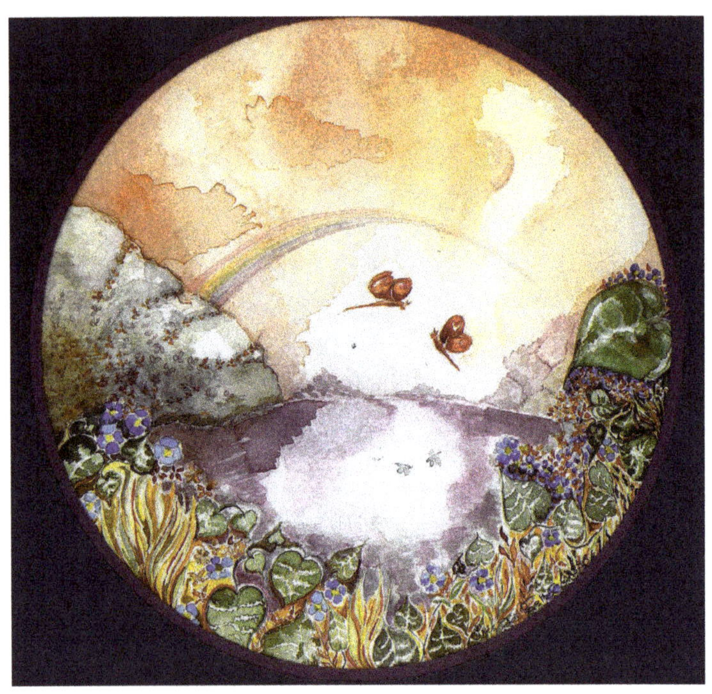

Love at First Sight, by Inés de Castro

Heaven is Calling

Heaven can sing,
heaven is calling.
Awaiting us
to be one—to be love!

When I was alone
in the bitterness of night
Could not think
Dared not hope …

But still I'd go!
With reason which blinds
and heavy heart
into darkness and pits …

Forever apart from light …

When all was lost,
I've seen the light!
For all that was darkened
has perished without sight!

I've seen you dance,
I've heard you sing
and flowers about your feet
were melting in love, blossoming!

And there I saw, there I knew!
Before time and all,
before the wailing of souls
I saw us standing above.

Your heart to mine
and mine to yours,
Our souls as one
Forevermore

Heaven can sing,
heaven is calling.
Awaiting us
to be one—to be love!

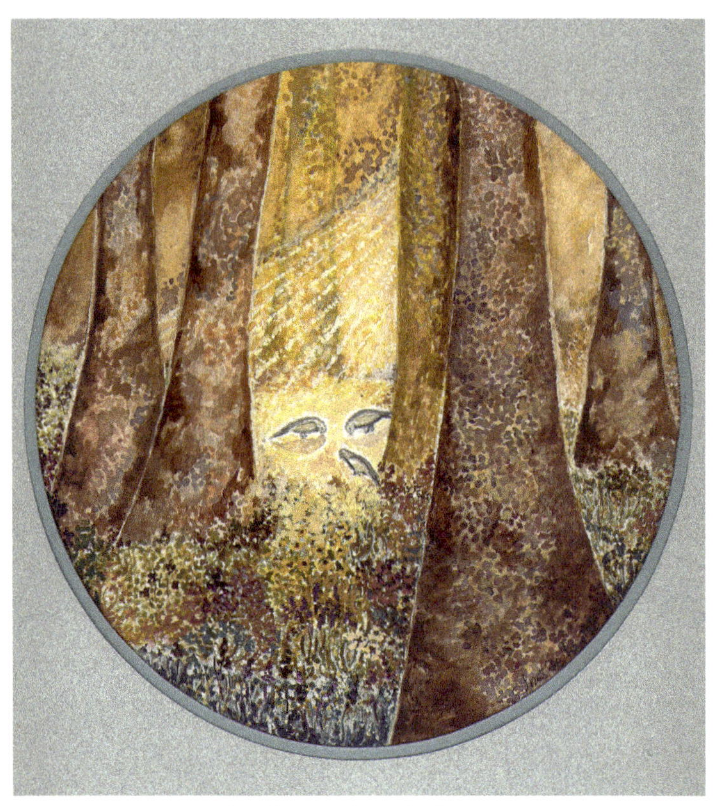

In the Clearing, by Inés de Castro

Beacon of Life

Darkness creeps in,
wearing a cloak of love, dawn and green.

Hearts are troubled 'cause they feel,
an unknown menace that is real.

Cast a light!
Lead the fight!

Love them 'till they die!

For there is a force they cannot bear,
and a power that is THE scare!

Love—that beacon of life.

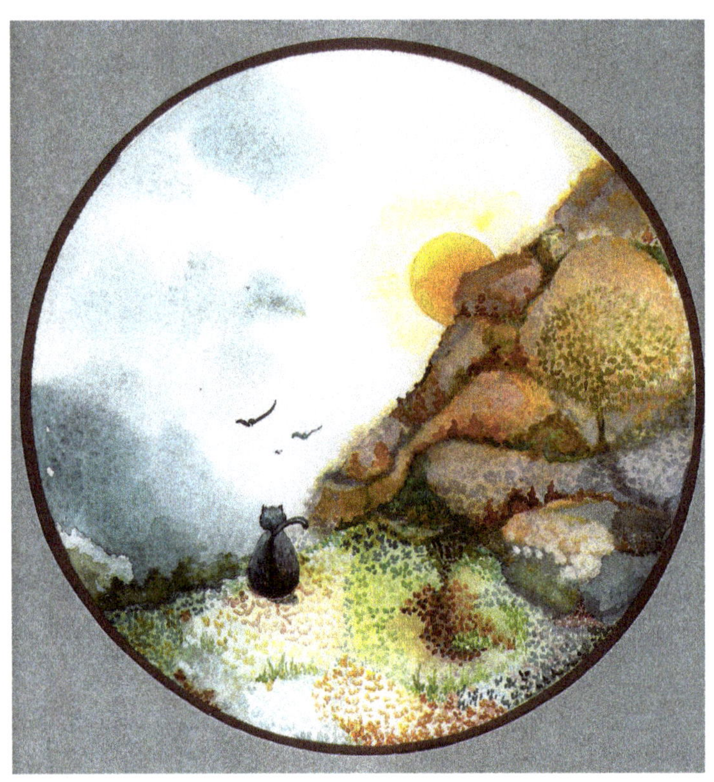

Rencontre, by Inés de Castro

Father Loves

Run out of time and feel right,
chase the winds of thoughts just to feel fine
and then when you close your eyes
when you drift along with all your hope
return back to love, to its golden slopes…

Never fear for the end is near!
Of illusion that tears apart righteous hearts.
But even this moment of flame will bring glory,
for everlasting moment—Love.

Now let's quit talking for words are tough.
Join me in the ride upon the nearest star,
Going high and flying far
only to be at home in our hearts.

Our Father is waiting, ever loving
for Love is forever and ever.
But now let's be!
And thank Him
for us, for all,
for He loves.

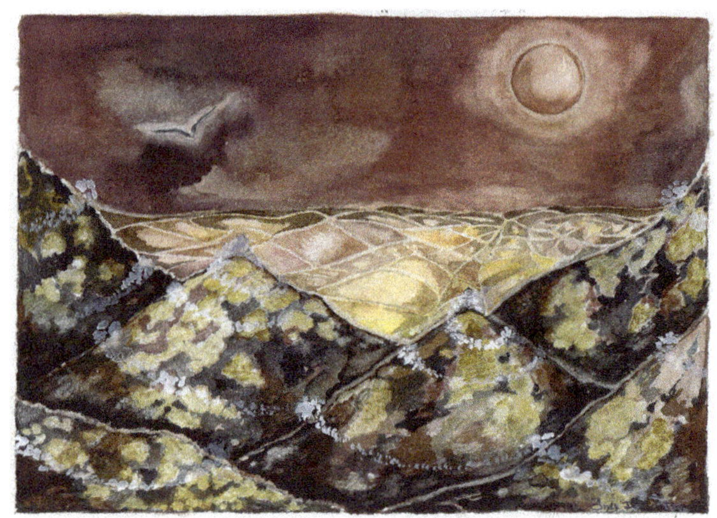

Night Dance, by Inés de Castro

Come Together

Come together!
Come now—tomorrow is too late …

Let us be there to shed a light …

Come together for there is power here!
As one we … we are love.

Come together, let us bathe in light!
Let us shrug off darkness, the dirty night.

But there is one thing you must do,
no excuse, all of you,

The first people your words did bite,
give them a little love, a little light.

Come together and don't say nay,
Tomorrow may be too late…

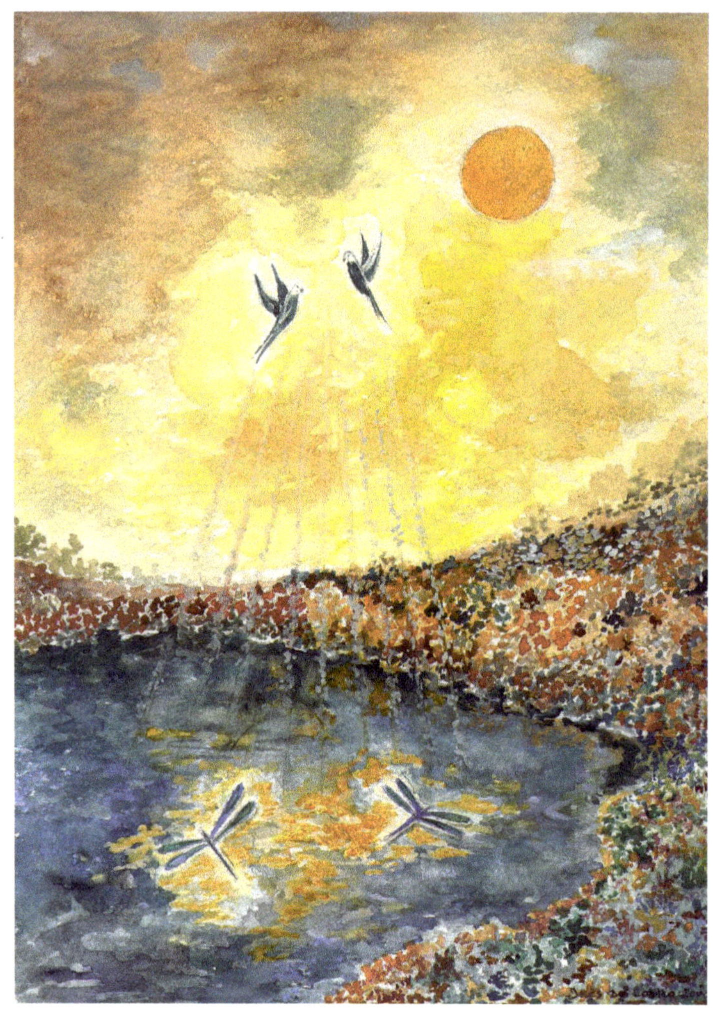

Duo, by Inés de Castro

Where my Soul is Free

I want to fly across open skies
be here or be there, wherever I so please
need to feel joy after endless tries
through dawns and dusks whom I always tease…

…whom I always tease to see
what will happen underneath every tree
when rains and mists bring life
and flowers take it up and readily spring out!

I want to see glorious waterfalls on the river that is small
and golden apples on the silver tree
beautiful colors of the rainbow
over the land where my soul is free…

Lilies

A river was gliding in silence in a valley where battle will be.

I see Lilies and green grass.
Dancing with wind…
Sun is making them smile — they shine!

… I see them in the mire, but just for a moment,
where glorious steeds will stand and just one voice will tear the air…!

Lilies are teasing my soul now.
Awakening thoughts which had been fading.
Images and scents of life, laugh and the one I love,
for whom I breathe…

… Trumpets and red sky!

Fingers are slipping over the flowers…
A Knight knelt down and talked to Lilies…
No one heard him, but the true heart knows his words.

Oh true heart!
Do you hear those words?

"Beloved one, I am coming here to die.
Where my rest shall be sweet, here among Lilies.
I am coming, my dear, because of Justice and Truth
which are fading in this world,
For the cry of innocent and sorrow of souls, O my
love...

"I know that battle would not be seen with eyes
but harder it is than anything under this sky!
I go now, beloved one.
Save one tear for me,
but of joy, not of sorrow!
Because your Knight has raised his sword for light!
For new day, for new tomorrow!

"And so I go to die here on this field of life and death
and Lilies,
and if it is the will of the Good Lord,
I will see you again my love.
Farewell."

I saw quiet river and green valley and warriors of light
how they ride glorious steeds!
And I saw the army of night ...
O how it is black...
It has surrounded the righteous camp.

The horse screamed and the warrior's sword blazed in the air!

Hey! Hey! Hey!

The Ground is shaking and earth weeps, weeps, weeps...

Hey! Hey!

Fiery blaze and anger are there in the knight's friends' eyes!

Hey!

The horse stomped and a hundred fell beneath him,

Hey!

...everywhere is dust and wind!

Hey!

Sword is high!

Hey!

Heads of the army of night are falling down,
left and right...
the road is being made through the bodies,
from the hands of warriors of light!

High in the air there was this tune:

“My brothers, don’t stop now—Hey!”
Sings the knight on glorious horse…
“No matter if they are countless
on this judgment day!”

“For truth—all!
Let love prevail!”

Roaring—Hey!

For the righteous God, my brothers–now!
Let the world of evil break down!”

Hey!

I saw the valley quiet and peaceful where the final battle was.
The grass lies down and there are no more flowers…
Vultures are flying over the bodies…

But there where the horse rider has stopped,
and a moment before a battle has talked,
there stands a flower alone above the breath of death.
It’s been teased by the breeze and the golden Sun.

The warriors are gone and their horses too.
There is no evil now, just shadow and a smoke of doom.

But that Lily is the only witness to that beloved woman,
it keeps the words of her Knight, her man.

From the wind that crashed all, the Good God kept it
because of that love.

And she takes it from the ground,
one tear fell from her eye,
that the eternal love may live inside her
which was kept for her Knight.

In the moment when she was losing herself inside,
squeezing the flower on her sore breasts,
the light shone through the fog on her!
And there were the figures of them!
Faster and faster
figures of those glorious heroes
who were fighting for love,
and her Knight how he rides towards her!

When she learned that it's just an illusion
of her pain,
something has turned her gaze to the sky, to the light!

And there she saw with her eyes,
one smile in her sunset,
because all the lives of that heroes, who died for justice
and truth, Good God does not forget,

And I saw again the field and golden valley,
and green grass and still waters…
and the smile of God who gave it all!
and her and him and Lilies,
blessed with everlasting love.

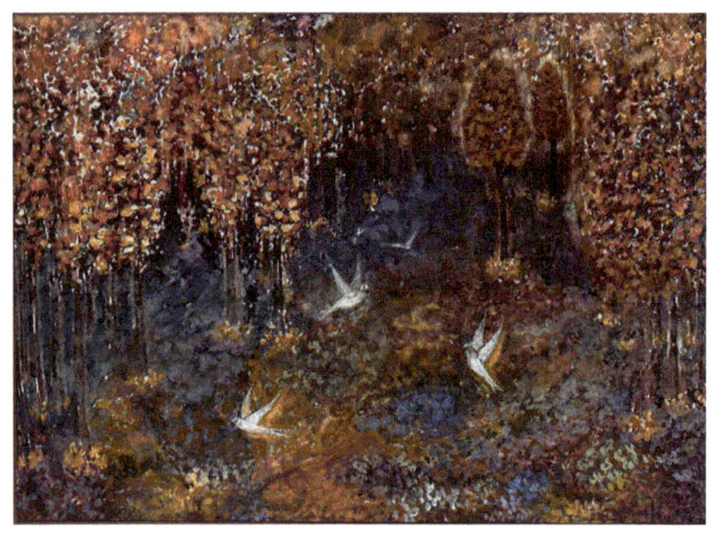

Between Friends, by Inés de Castro

Hunter

The hour grows late…
Racket around us and blinding hate…

Smoke of doom lies across,
and open eyes filled with lust
tantrums and violence!

I choose to deafen my ears from this noise!
I will not give it life,
not even a choice!

For a long time has now passed
since my peace was broken.
Now I fight back!

As they stalked me with hate,
in gloomy hours of night,
I will pierce them with love,
for they cannot bear that!

I will be as mad as man can be,
I will not rest until I hunt them down,
hunt them down like ravaging wolves,
in their caves filled with lust.

Ever behind their steps…
I will be the haunter yes!
I will shine with love,
more—as they care less!

They will growl and moan with pain.
But this is my hour and my gain!

They shoot with darkness and I with love,
We'll see whom they threatened with fires below!

I stand alone but alone I am not!
my heavenly Father loves me
and gives hope.

Ere the just tomorrow rise
to forever banish darkness,

Light, love and truth will guide you
above evil, every madness…

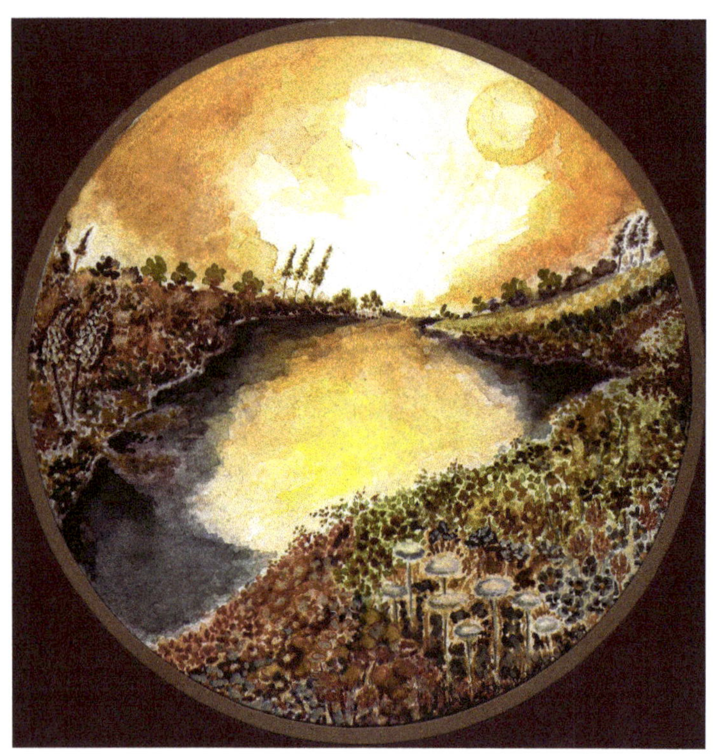

Golden River, by Inés de Castro

Remember

Days are getting shorter and thoughts bigger
and I am dreaming in the broad daylight
of everlasting Spring…

I remember the time when beauty was
all around us, in the forest of Birch trees
where nightingales sing.

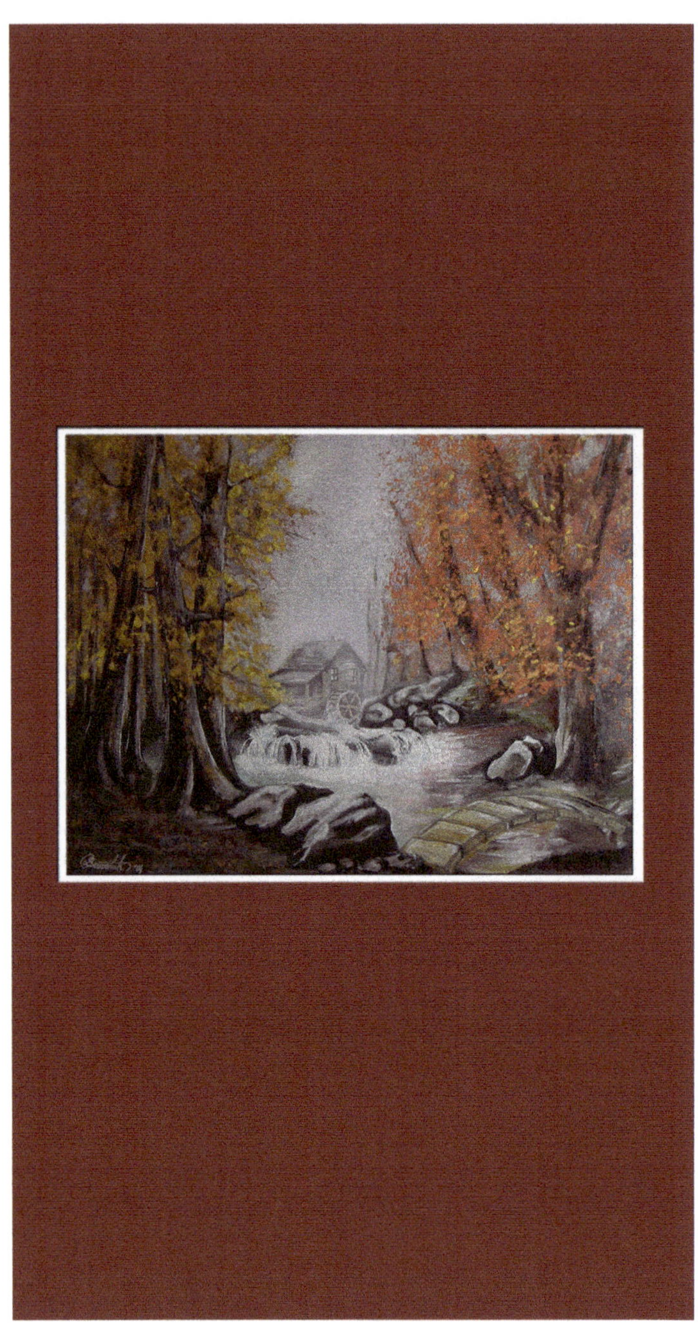

Coming Home, by Dalibor Zlatkovic

Coming Home

Many miles are under my feet…
cold stones and dust that covers.

Many miles are still waiting for me,
silver trees and violet flowers…

Oh how silence is loud sometimes,
In the darkest hours of my heart!

But tomorrow a new Sun rises…
Another mile will be long gone,

Listening to the bird's song which praises,
carrying my bags filled with love.

Leaving behind yesterday's gray,
heading towards glorious day!
I'm coming home…

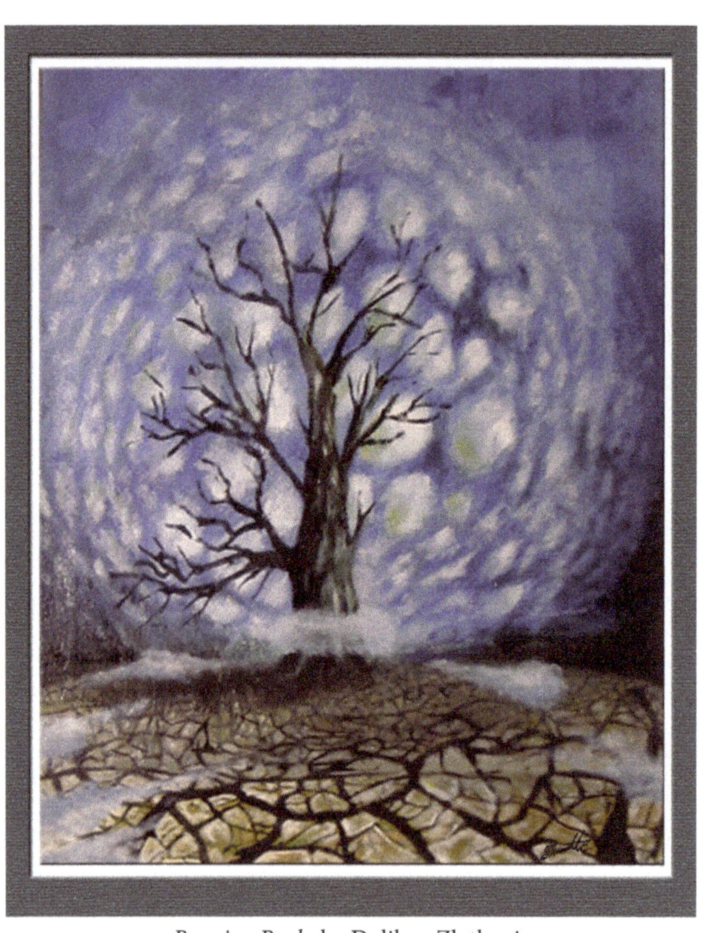

Burning Bush, by Dalibor Zlatkovic

Love is God

Light as a butterfly and heavy as the universe!
Gentle as a woman can be
and harsh as icy wind…

Turn it around,
up and down—you'll see nothing,
you'll hear no sound.

Try to catch it
quickly smash it!
But only air you'll feel,
my friend…

If only your eyes can see
through the mist of thought,
perfectly clear…

If only your ears can hear
above sounds of war,
over the tears!

If only your fingers can touch it,
under its surface
behind the padlocked door…

Inside of you and outside of you,
everywhere…
Here and there, in and out of your soul.

and through the hate…
—where is love???

Is it in the air,
in the sky,
deep below the arctic night…
on high peaks of misty mountains
or in the fiery abyss
deep in its fountains???
Where does it lie?
Where does it stand?

And then…in the moment the touch of light
an overwhelming wave!

Life is at grasp of your hand,
Love is God
God is Love.

Open your heart and let love in,
let it in now—soon it will be too late
because some live just to hate!
Some are living just to die
or taking other lives, never saying why…

For truth—open your soul now,
for there is no power or force but love!

And then when you look to the sky
you will just know,
that Love is God
that God is Love.

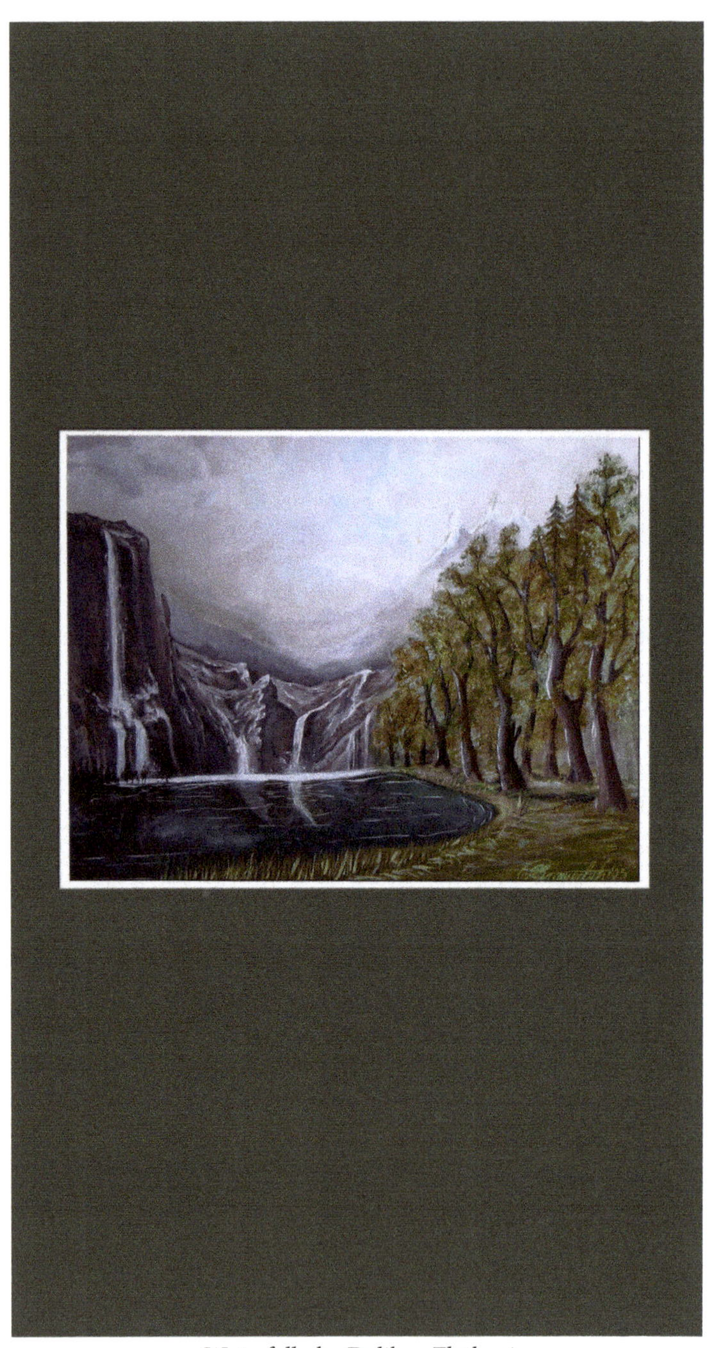

Waterfalls, by Dalibor Zlatkovic

Poet

It is easy to say rhyme and verse,
and beautiful song lights sparkle in the eye!
But to paint gentle words of the heart
and sing about love is a gift from the sky…

Raise your Swords

Let us together raise our swords in this fight…
Since we are on the side that will beat the night!

Those are swords of truth, of light and love,
as above so below!

Our fight is not seen with eyes and many will not care,
but our task and our core of heartbeat is to dare!

To dare to live, and dare to love,
so tell me who can beat us then and now?

With a look towards blue skies,
I am sending you my will and grace
and everlasting peace, now…

Riders of the Storm

I am fighting with this lightning,
It's burning my hands…

Will you help me, my friend of old?
I cannot wield alone this bolt!

Other friends will come along
in their ways into this world…

We'll be riding the storm
with sheer joy!

It is burning our hands but warming our hearts,
we're shedding light over dark skies!

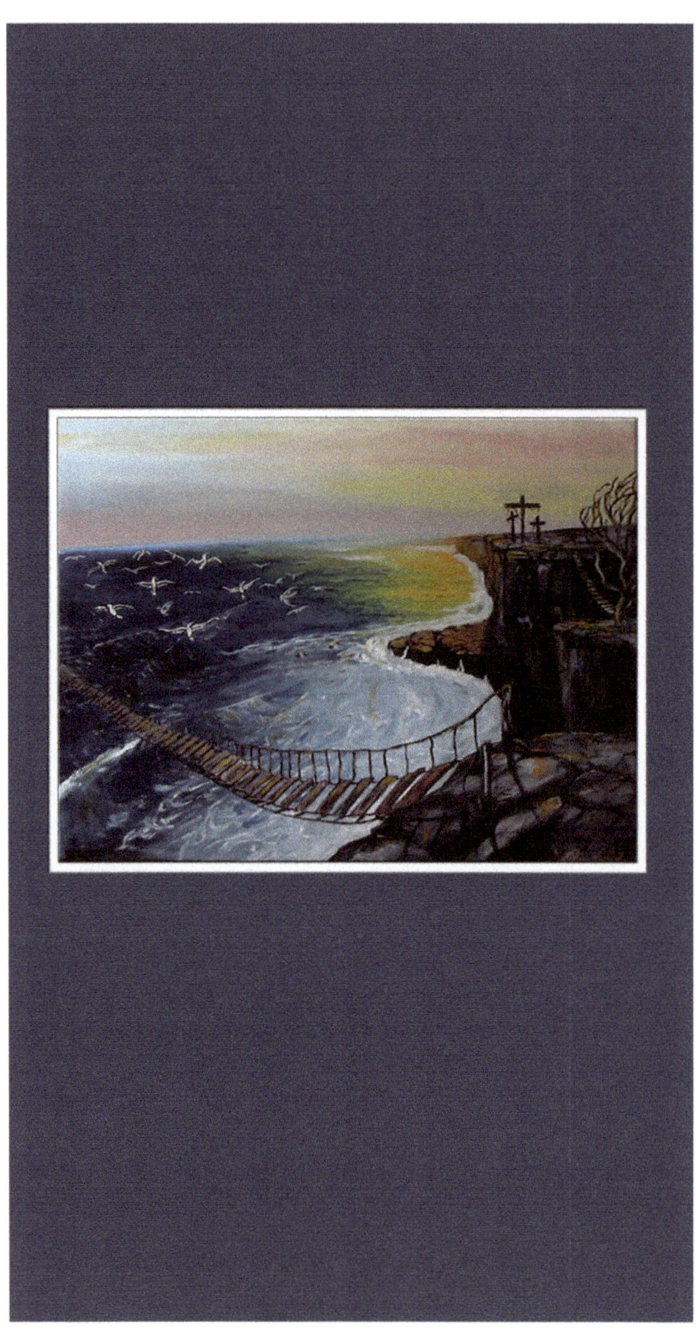

The Bridge, by Dalibor Zlatkovic

Scent of Divine

For whom do all flowers bloom?
Is it not for the eyes of the beholder?

For whom do they carry the scent of the Divine?
for my heart and thine…

For whom little lily opens its chest,
when dawn brings in the champagne of moisture?

It takes a minute, maybe a day…
and a whole eternity to be carried away!

Into heavenly realms,
our Father's playgrounds…

To grasp the beauty of one flower,
created for us and all others…

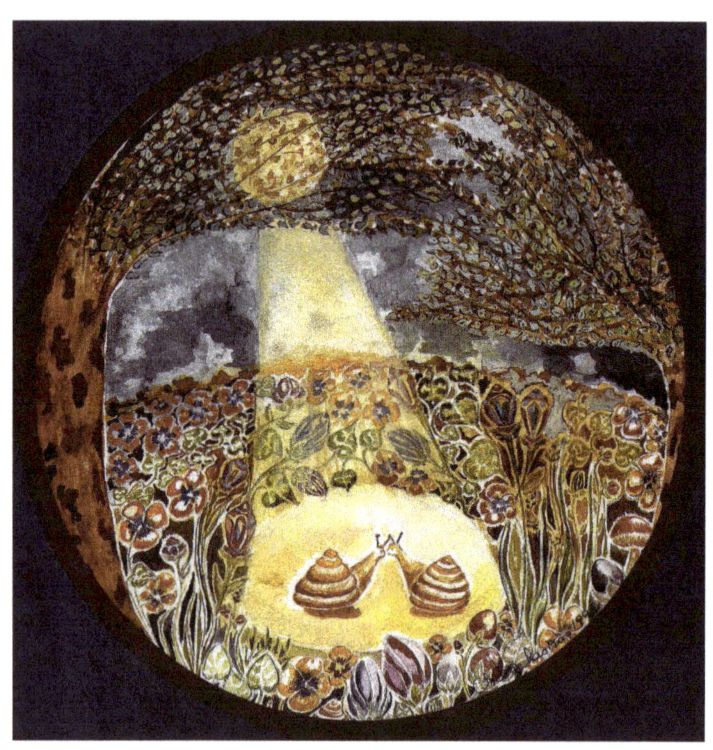

Le mariage des escargots, by Inés de Castro

Stargazer

Minstrels are singing loudly,
for darkness is conquered by light!

A new age is dawning brave,
where all are humans,
where there are no slaves.

Words cannot say and eyes cannot see,
all that is carried by light—nay!
Towards our hearts, our very souls
in this day.

And I am no longer just a Stargazer,
because the dream I live again.
For through the spirit I see the Maker,
in this glorious day!

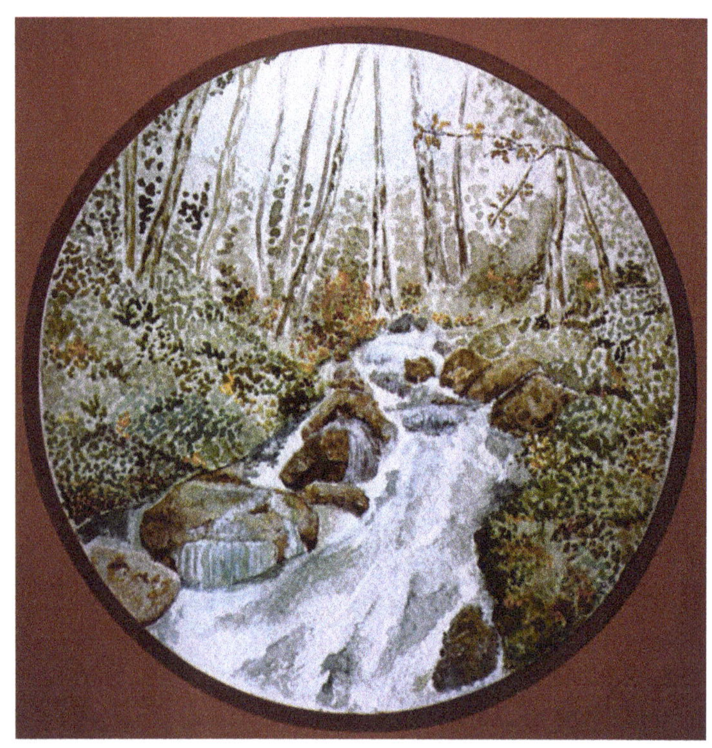

Cascade, by Inés de Castro

Words are Not Enough

Sometimes words are not enough;
sometimes I'd paint a picture and in the middle of it I'd
place nothing…

I would be lost within reality since I cannot transcribe it
to you…

All can fit in a dot of space and
that dot would be bigger than Earth…

I want to sail together with birds, on mighty winds…
to gaze on everything
from above…
to see the place where you and I were born,
to bless it with love…

Oh how I want that!

Then I am there in the forest of old.
There my eyes saw the beauty.
I stepped on the hemlock
and lost my heart forever…

She took it away…with gentle voice, gentle soul.

Her hair was playing with breeze and singing she was…

She would tease the flowers,
gently…
and they would follow, stretching their tiny heads a bit,
giving her heavenly scent,
as a present…

Oh my eyes, fool me not this time!
Fool me not since I wish to make you open all the time
…
to see this woman forever…

Dark have been my dreams of late,
full of sorrow, sadness, hate.

Until I wandered or was led,
to this forest, to my dream—can't forget!

Lutien, I still hear your song in my mind…
It's taking me away, away…

To a beautiful place somewhere in time,
Where I live love, where I stay…

With you, my love…

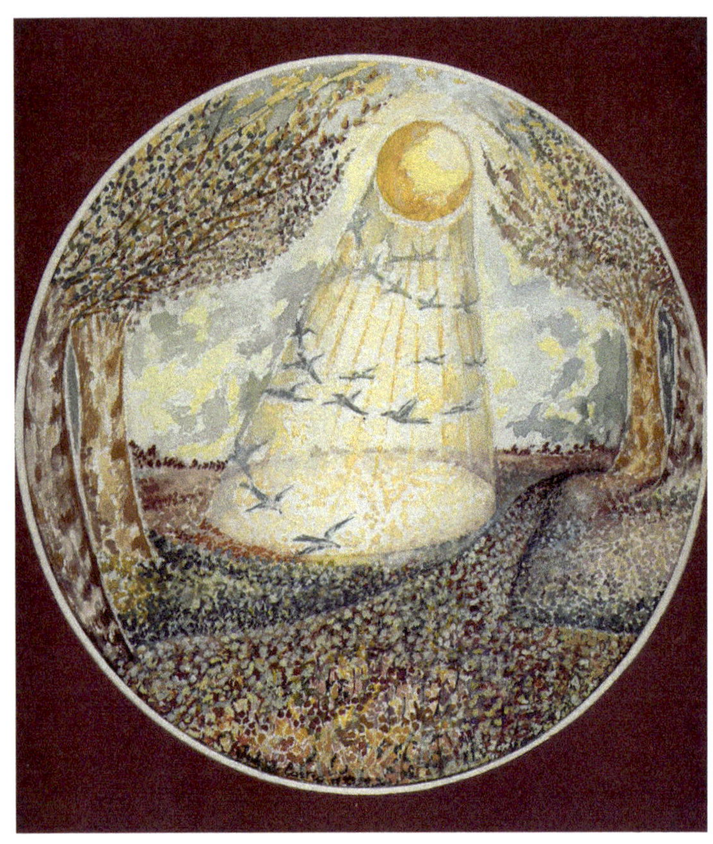

Rounding, by Inés de Castro

Here and Now

Here and now our fate is being made!
Either a flower or plain dust—no one can fake.

And day carries on…
Sometimes golden dawn
but sometimes blunt rain.

But the question always remains the same.
Will it be in Love or in vain?
For always we create,
In cherished Love or in blind hate.

My World

Riding the wild wind
sheer joy
adrenaline.

And in the evening
sipping tea
wondering and believing

in all good living things before me
green hills
and white lily.

And then the night!
wonders of the glorious sky!
sprinkled all over
The Stars, Stars!

A new day and I am amazed
again!
For new things were created
from my friends!

Tiny greens and lustrous waters
pink roses
new wonders!

And my clothes are gone!
Bare naked I lie down,
but not ashamed!

For Lutien was there
weaving for me new threads
and sparkling they are!

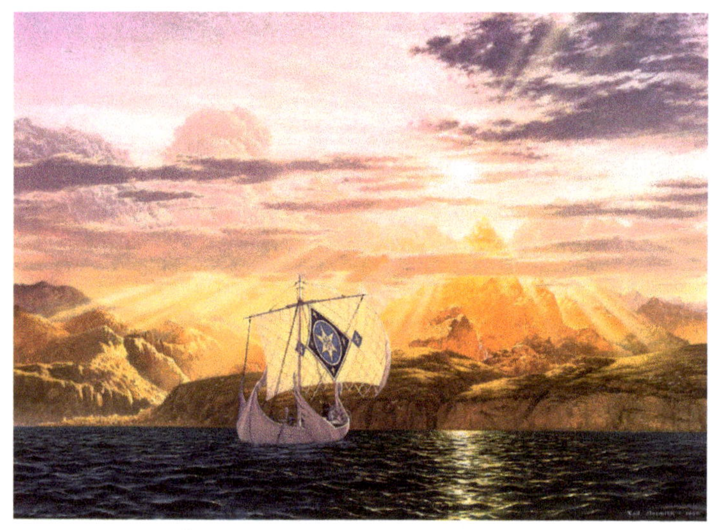

The Shores of Valinor, by Ted Nasmith

My Beautiful Father

I need to thank you, I must,
my beautiful Father.

For all the life that I feel,
because there is no other…

No one greater whom I can trust
In the vastness of the universe,
In all thoughts that exist
you are there because YOU live…

For every breath that I take
and everything that I do
for all my senses and all I make
I yearn to say "thank you…"

And I bless you and I love you.

And I ask you to send your blessing
across the lands, across the space
that every soul who feels the light
may grow in grace!

That's why I need to thank you,
my dear Father in heaven,
For love is all there is,
let it shine - now and forever!

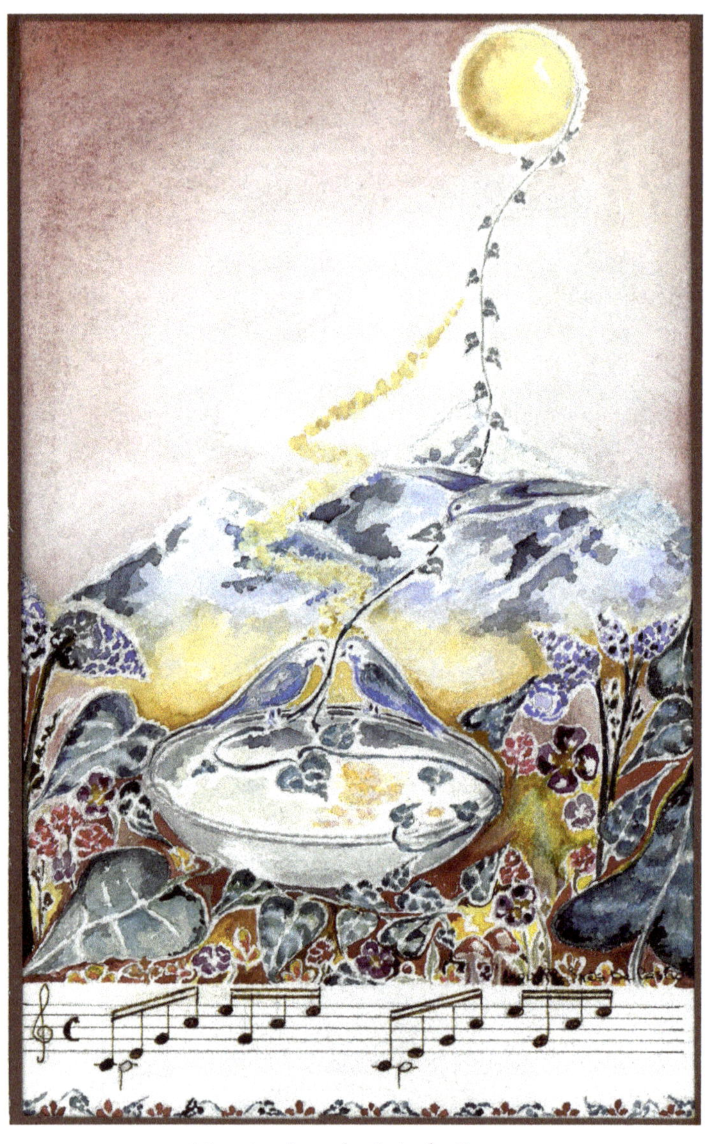

Morning Song, by Inés de Castro

Song of Power

I sing a song of power.
From old days which are new
from forgotten streams and wild peaks
and valleys that bring morning dew…

O how we marched straight to the very gates of doom!
Across the plain and wild lakes
To face the looming gloom

and stood against fiery drakes!

Stood tall and sang brave!
Mocking fear and its open grave.
Love in our sails
and hope in our veins!!!

I sing a song of power
Now and forever!

Never Fear

I want to be the light
here and now!
Heard a voice inside…
Light that shatters darkness and
brings new dawns!

Because I want to go home…
where I belong, where I love
and am being loved.
Where yesterday is now and tomorrow too.

And I am going home,
but before I lay my foot on the road,
before my heart rejoices in the scene
that I see, that I feel…
I am here.

And I am raising my sword!
made of sheer God's word,
standing quite alone
among the hordes of drones.

They don't feel and they are blind,
for all that moves through the light…
and there my plan lies
to shine and shine!
To love and cry!

To cry a shout that will shatter out!
looking up and seeing far
through the mists, darkened hearts
singing a tune of light!

Through the night of my soul
I voyaged far and wide,
saw the worlds, through the universe…
On a never-ending quest for peace…
peace for all my brothers, sisters out there …

Never fear!
The End of darkness is very near.
It is time and time is now,
to return back to the Love.

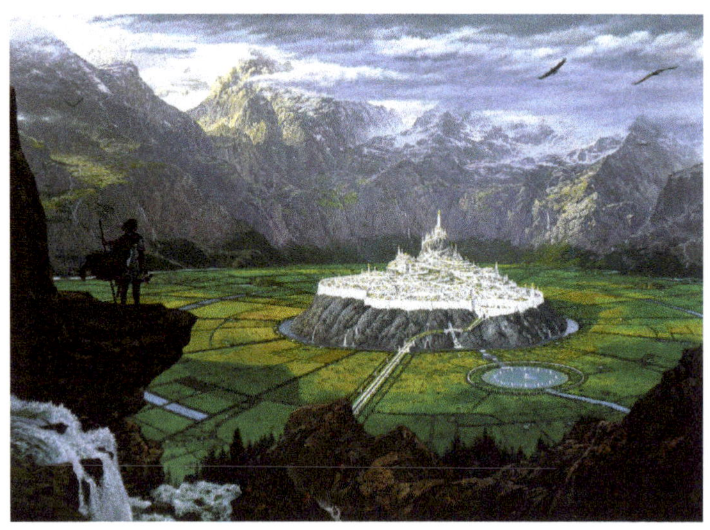

Tuor Reaches the Hidden City of Gondolin, by Ted Nasmith

Can you Feel My Love?

My child, can you feel my Love?
Asked once I was…

In everything that is around you
in all that surrounds you?

In glorious starry sky
and tiny leaf of birch tree
in autumn passing by?

I can feel your Love…
now…

I can see with eyes of the soul
where lies my true home…

In your gardens beside living pool
and trees of life

I see your Love
for Love …it is You!

Wordsmith

Come to me, here.
And I will tell you of many things;
of beauty and how it fell
and darkness and its tale.

And a long story it will be
For words are the weak link,
for it is hard to paint the picture
to weave the thread of all deeds.

But stand fast!
Arm yourself with patience
and stand your ground
for many hidden things lie there to be found.

Things that scare and things that dare
Things that open the soul apart
and soothing balm upon your inner heart
are they…

It all began with a thought
Of splendor!
Of Love!
Of Light and much more!

And then it exploded into rays of light and sheer joy
A wave that carries all.
Stream of love and conscious joy.
When ages have begun.

Though many words can be awoken
and many here to speak be called,
I will not say much now
For I send you my Love.

And I send it with light,
go play it in your heart.
for its beauty will now spring
singing to you of many things
and thousands of words,
that you need to know…

Wordsmithing is an honorable craft,
and indeed I was blessed for that.
But one thing that my heart wants
is to share this light, this true Love.

For one picture is worth a thousand words!
And I am painting now with the color of Love…
So stand your ground
for the longest tale
that exists out there,
and in here —
in our hearts.

Quiet Are the Ways of the Lord

Quiet are the ways of the Lord,
for He builds in great splendor!
You can't hear and you can't see…

Indeed those are ways of glory,
the spark is blazing the hearts of you and me,
so we can feel and hear and see.

And blue we feel living down here,
running far and going nowhere.
Fighting that mighty sea…

That great sea of power,
which has brought us lower
than we are,
than we really are…

O my, O my!

Can I say a word to you
and your friends and their friends too?

For I shed the unseen tear
for brothers and sisters far and near…

And yet only stillness do I hear…

For quiet are the ways of the Lord
for He works in great splendor!
May we listen,
may we hear…
What is coming very near
to all hearts that are beating right!

May we see!
Love and glory!

For quiet were the ways of the Lord,
for now we hear his voice in splendor!

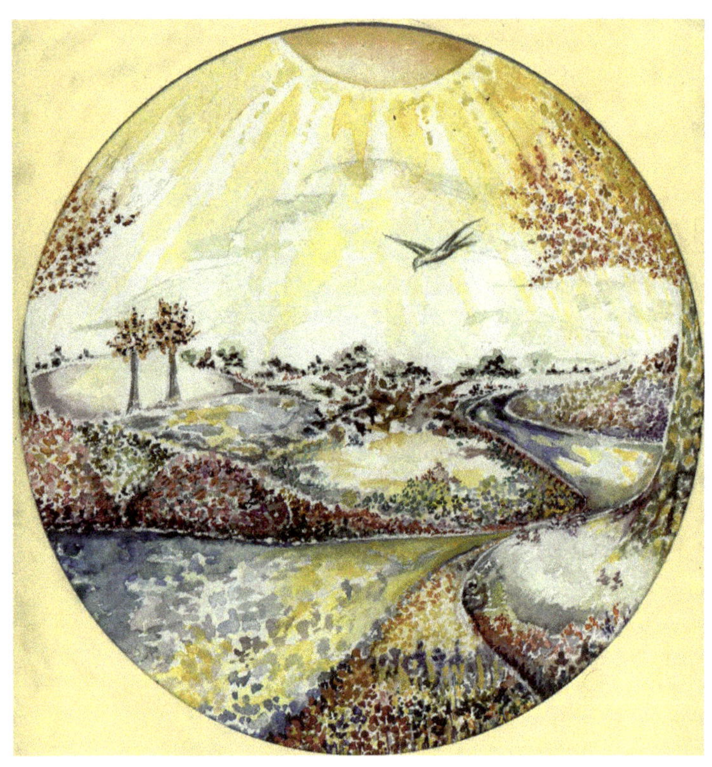

Visit to China, by Inés de Castro

I Bless

I bless the day I saw your eyes,
I bless the time we had together,
time before time
and love before world.

Now I am here to set some things
but my heart stayed with you,
forever bound to create and love
and fill with light, peace and truth.

I blessed the day when Father stood by me
and open arms of all in song,
I bless the day that stands before us
in light, in truth, in Love.

Blessed Be

Long ago in times and ages forgotten now,
I stood on the green hill, gazed upon the stars
was silent, for amazement
beyond measure was in my heart…

For I saw the hand of God at work!
The Fairest of all, walked on this beautiful Earth,
Blessed Lutien Tinuviyel…
Whom I love.

Long ago I saw that beauty and talked with Father.
And no one saw our faces joining together, weaving
beauty, weaving Love.

And Father told me of unseen things yet to awaken,
across the lands of universe and beautiful lakes…
Of life and streams of Love
in dimensions unseen below and above…

I am here now to tell you about Love,
to weave my words like a beautiful poem.
The very words that Father taught me
Of pearls in heaven and gates of Love.

And who knows but Father where we will go next,
unless He reveals his love upon our chests…
Therefore I bless him forever!
And all dear souls that I see whenever,

whenever I open my eyes and hear the song,
of all beloved souls that walk upon,
upon beautiful hills of distant lands…
And this Earth beneath our soles.

Blessed be my dear friend of old
I have found you along with many,
journeying far,
traveling bold.

Blessed be and filled with Love
And I ask the Father to share his love,
For you and with you always
Shine now and be Love.

Above the Mists

What is a river if not a playing thing?
what is a flower if not shared?
what is beauty if not seen?

In the playground for God's children
there is only Love.
And nothing but life.

I heard a word from a little girl
about beauty unchained
ever new, ever fresh…

and vision appeared as bright as Sun
that gentleness is the new dawn,
the smooth way of the heart,

And the silky way of a soul…

For there is only one goal:
for all that exist
to sing a new tune

of creation above the mists…

And what is a field of Lilies if I am alone there?
And what is a river if I swim alone there?
And what is a flower if I smell it alone there?

Just a picture without a frame
a song without a name
a cool breeze on a cold day.

So that's why I sail
over vast horizons of life
ever with light on my face!

I give you my hand
I give you my heart
treat them as you would yourself, as God.

Sacred are the ways of Love
ever changing its tune but never repeating the same
blues
that we lived down here…

So we shall sing!
Glorious new beginning,
of life as it is and as it will be.

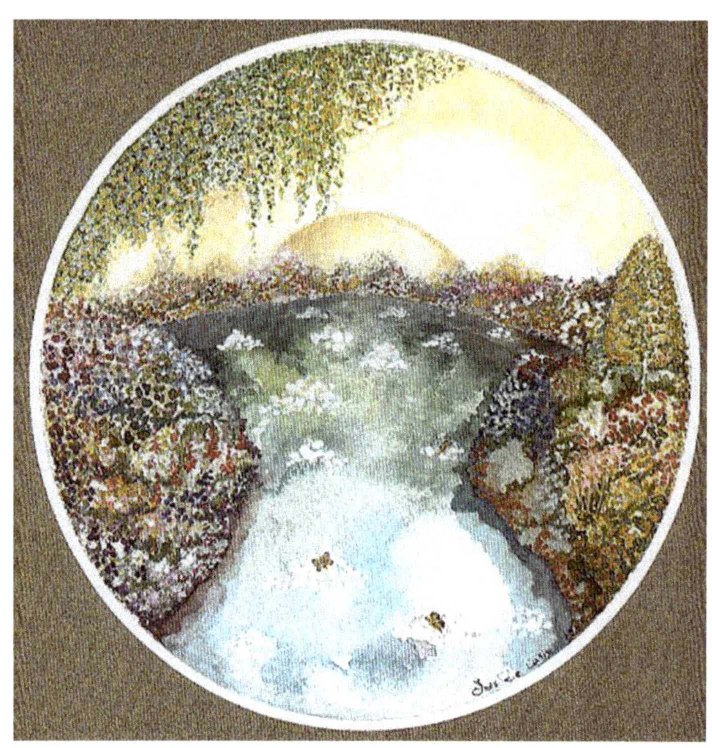

East of Eden, by Inés de Castro

From the Forgotten World into Eternity

From the forgotten world into eternity
comes a vibration of clarity
ever present, forevermore
a mighty sound, color, lore.

But as gentle as the breeze
in the midsummer starry eve...

And no word of human tongue
can paint its glory now
restless forever and peaceful now
breath, power, soul—Love

Some will say join me here,
we are making a new world
project your mind into vastness of space
seek and find all with your heart
be part of a new human race!

I stand alone.

But alone I am not.
Before the thought of new horizons came
into hearts and mind to reign,
I sang a song of beauty and love.

Father stood beside me and smiled.
Tinuviyel on left so full of light…
And then words were straight!
"Ye will go and new things make."

And here I am singing it now!
Blessed be O Father Love!
Forever is now!
from the forgotten world
into eternity
with Love.

About the Artists

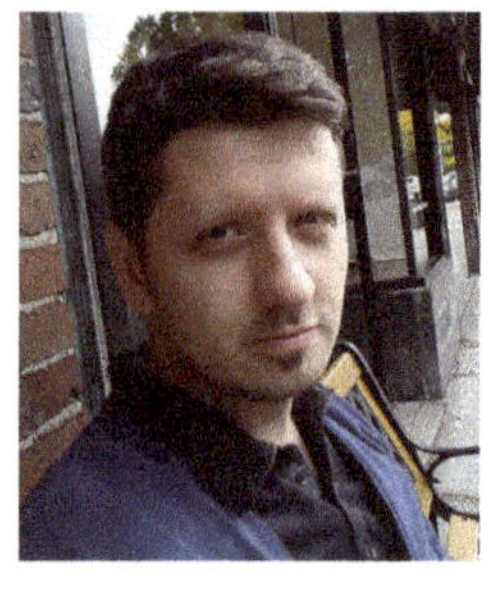

Beren Maximus is the *nom de plume* of **Milorad Maksimovic**. Born in Belgrade, Serbia, he began writing poety at an early age, first in Serbian and later also in English. "Flashes of light and myself traveling through unknown quantum field of experience catching phrases shapes colors and … things … just to channel them into words that became poems.

"Divine beauty was and is always there for all to see and feel it —just one quick brush over your eyes and voila! It's there. Your own treasure. Your own life and love. "I live art in all ways and enjoy art in all forms. I hope that my art will touch hearts and inspire souls to find their own treasure and shine it forth!"

Milo now lives and works in Massachusetts, USA. His website and blog can be found at www.fromforgottenworld.com/

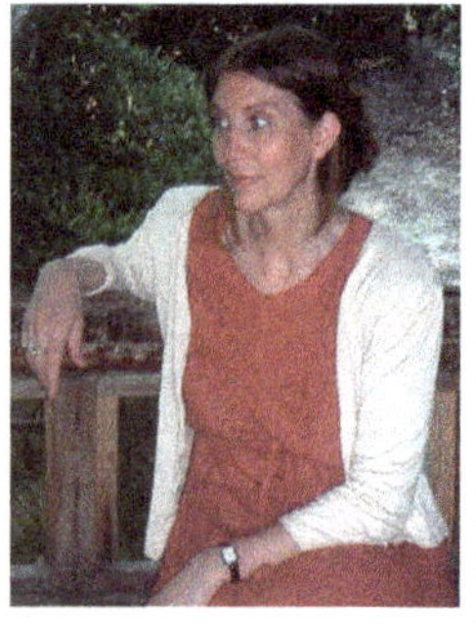

Inés De Castro is a Belgian artist born in Ghent, Belgium, in 1954. She sometimes paints under the name "Mudra."

From early childhood she would spend hours in contemplation in various gardens and fields. There she sat quietly in silence being receptive to nature's whispers.

Her art reflects the peace she found in those moments of deep connection to the sacred beyond words. As she was gazing at a particular painting, her daughter Laura once expressed her wish to enter that space and visit these enchanted lands of flowers, trees, mushrooms, butterflies, birds. "How wonderful, her innocent eyes understood at first sight these circle paintings of mine are indeed so many vistas inviting you, the beholder, to another world, the forgotten world…"

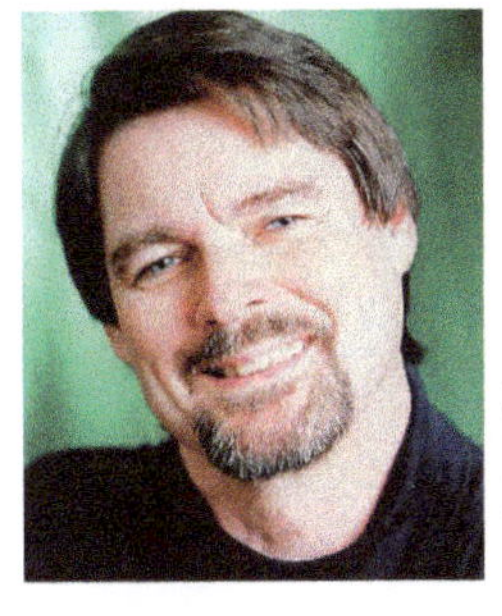

Ted Nasmith is a Canadian artist, illustrator and former architectural renderer. He is best known as an illustrator of J. R. R. Tolkien's works — *The Hobbit*, *The Lord of the Rings* and *The Silmarillion*. Nasmith was born in the mid-1950s in Goderich, Ontario, Canada.

As the son of a Royal Canadian Air Force electronics technologist, Nasmith's early life was characterized by a series of moves as his father was re-assigned during his military career. Nasmith's family and friends encouraged him to enter a high school which featured a commercial art program.

During his third year of high school, however, Nasmith's sister introduced him to *The Lord of the Rings*, and it quickly became a huge inspiration and focus in his life. Nasmith writes: "It opened up in me a dormant love of lost and misty times, myth and legend. Not since childhood had I felt such a sense of 'home', unaware of the effects the intervening years had had in displacing it. I began immediately to draw scenes inspired by this magical, nostalgic realm, becoming absorbed for many hours at a time." (Nasmith 2002)

In recent years Nasmith has added illustrations for the bestselling George R. R. Martin novels *A Song of Ice and Fire* to his continuing work as a fantasy illustrator.

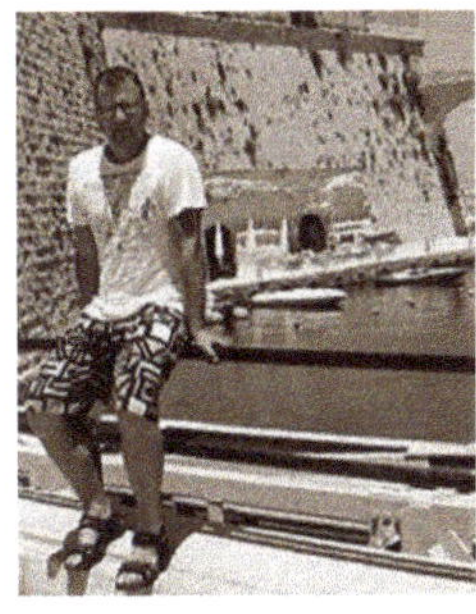

Dalibor Zlatkovic was born in Vlasotince, Serbia. Since his early childhood he has shown a great interest in art. Intrigued by many prominent artists, he has created a unique point of view representing art as a multifunctional system which helps one's soul to survive in this age. Even though he graduated from the College for Professional Studies of Belgrade Polytechnics as a graphics designer, he remains keenly interested in painting and photography.

Illustrations

www.ingramcontent.com/pod-product-compliance
Lightning Source LLC
LaVergne TN
LVHW052355100826
845147LV00013B/851